INSPiRE

CAITLIN CLARK

BY KIM THOMPSON

AMICUS LEARNING

Inspire is published by
Amicus Learning, an imprint of Amicus
P.O. Box 227
Mankato, MN 56002
www.amicuspublishing.us

Editor: Ana Brauer
Series Designer: Kathleen Petelinsek
Book Designer: Rhea Magaro

Library of Congress Cataloging-in-Publication Data
Names: Thompson, Kim, 1970- author.
Title: Caitlin Clark / by Kim Thompson.
Description: Mankato, MN : Amicus Learning, 2025. | Series: Inspire | Includes bibliographical references and index. | Audience: Ages 5–9 | Audience: Grades 2–3 | Summary: "Learn about WNBA star Caitlin Clark in an engaging biography packed with action photos and fact-filled text. Elementary sports fans will learn about Clark's childhood, her record-breaking college basketball career, and her rookie year with the Indiana Fever. Includes table of contents, glossary, further resources, and index"— Provided by publisher.
Identifiers: LCCN 2024035642 (print) | LCCN 2024035643 (ebook) | ISBN 9798892006323 (library binding) | ISBN 9798892006347 (paperback) | ISBN 9798892006361 (ebook)
Subjects: LCSH: Clark, Caitlin, 2002-—Juvenile literature. | Women basketball players—United States—Biography—Juvenile literature.
Classification: LCC GV884.C554 T56 2025 (print) | LCC GV884.C554 (ebook) | DDC 796.323092 [B]—dc23/eng/20240805
LC record available at https://lccn.loc.gov/2024035642
LC ebook record available at https://lccn.loc.gov/2024035643

Photo Credits: Alamy Stock Photo/ZUMA Press, 15; Associated Press/Erica Denhoff/Icon Sportswire, cover, Brian Spurlock/Icon Sportswire, 12, Adam Hunger, 18; Getty Images/Emilee Chin, 5, Scott Taetsch, 6, Luke Hales, 8, Diamond Images, 11, David K Purdy, 17, Chris Coduto, 19, 20-21

Printed in the United States of America

Table of Contents

Playmaker

Caitlin Clark plays in the Women's National Basketball Association (WNBA). Her team is the Indiana Fever. The star knows how to make plays. She passes to teammates. She shoots from the middle of the **court**. The ball goes in the basket. Three points!

LOGO 3s

Clark makes logo 3 shots. They are taken from the center of the court where the team logo is painted on the floor. They are worth three points.

Clark is a popular player. She has brought new fans to the WNBA.

From left: mom Anne Nizzi-Clark, dad Brent Clark, Caitlin, little brother Colin, big brother Blake

A Family That Plays Together

Clark is from Des Moines, Iowa. She grew up with her mom, dad, and two brothers. The whole family likes sports. Her dad played basketball in college. Her brothers are good at basketball and football.

SUPPORT SYSTEM

Clark leans on her family for support. She talks to her mom every day. Her dad and brothers encourage her and give advice.

Clark wants to inspire girls and boys to follow their dreams.

The Only Girl

Clark played sports at home with her brothers. She was always very **competitive**.

Sometimes, Clark played on boys' teams. She was often the only girl. She did not think much about it. She just wanted to win.

High School Star

Clark played soccer in high school. But she liked playing basketball best. She was a star player. By the 10th grade, college teams noticed her. In the 11th and 12th grades, she was Iowa Player of the Year.

RECORD-BREAKER

In one high school game, Clark made 13 three-point shots. It set a state record.

As a teenager, Clark joined the youth team All Iowa Attack to develop her skills.

Clark said, "I wouldn't be who I am if it wasn't for my coaches and my teammates."

A Hawkeye

Clark went to the University of Iowa. Her first year was during the COVID-19 outbreak. Not many fans came to Hawkeyes games. That took the pressure off. Clark **bonded** with her team. She became a better player.

Triple-Doubles

Clark was a great college player. She had 17 triple-doubles as a Hawkeye. That means she got double-digit scores in three areas like shooting, **assists**, and **rebounds**. Every time Clark got a triple-double, Iowa won the game.

HONORED

Clark was a First Team All-American three times. It is one of the highest honors for college players.

With Purdue players all around, Clark jumps to capture the ball for Iowa.

MAKERS
10 22 23 33 55 13
4 25 33 50 3 23
27 13 7 23
19 32 35 43 42
33
20
3
IOWA
OFFICIAL SPONS
PURD ATHL

Top Scorer

In four years of college, Clark played 130 games. She scored 3,685 points. She broke the record for the most points scored by a college player. The old record holder was Pete Maravich.

NICKNAME

People called Pete Maravich "Pistol Pete." After breaking his record, Clark got the nickname "Ponytail Pete."

In college, Clark scored more than 28 points per game.

WNBA Commissioner Cathy Engelbert announced Clark's new team.

Going Pro

After college, Clark joined a pro team. She was the Indiana Fever's first pick. Clark had a great first year with the Fever. She played on the WNBA All-Star Team. She was named **Rookie** of the Year.

HER HERO

As a kid, Clark looked up to WNBA player Brittney Griner. When the Indiana Fever played the Phoenix Mercury, Clark got to play against her idol.

Passing Pride

Clark is a star shooter. But she does not hog the ball. She is proud to pass to teammates. In 2024, she broke the WNBA record for assists. She had 337 in one season.

SUPER STATS

CAITLIN CLARK

Born: January 22, 2002

Birthplace: Des Moines, Iowa

Current Team: Indiana Fever

Position: Guard

AWARDS

AP Player of the Year: 2023, 2024

Big Ten Player of the Year: 2022, 2023, 2024

ESPYS Award, Best College Athlete, Women's Sports: 2023, 2024

ESPYS Award, Best Record-Breaking Performance: 2024

John R. Wooden Award: 2023, 2024

Naismith Women's College Player of the Year: 2023, 2024

Wade Trophy: 2023, 2024

WNBA Rookie of the Year: 2024

GLOSSARY

assist A pass of the ball to teammates that leads to scoring points.

bond To become close; to become good friends.

competitive Determined to win.

court A rectangular surface with a basket at each end where the game of basketball is played.

rebound A time when a player gets a ball that someone from the other team shot and missed.

rookie A player in their first year with the league.

READ MORE

Chandler, Matt. **Basketball Biographies for Kids: The Greatest NBA and WNBA Players from the 1960s to Today.** New York: Callisto Kids, 2022.

Hewson, Anthony K. **Caitlin Clark: Basketball Superstar.** Mendota Heights, Minn.: North Star Editions, 2024.

Sports Illustrated Kids. **Big Book of WHO: Women in Sports.** New York: Sports Illustrated, 2024.

ON THE WEB

Caitlin Clark Foundation
https://caitlinclarkfoundation.org

Indiana Fever
https://fever.wnba.com

WNBA – Caitlin Clark
https://www.wnba.com/player/1642286/caitlin-clark

INDEX

About the Author

Kim Thompson is a teacher and writer from Columbus, Ohio. She is a big basketball fan. She loves it when a close game gets exciting and the arena gets loud. She cheers and stomps her feet with the rest of the crowd.